Reader Notice:

The Reveal

Being permitted to peek into someone's heart
May be somewhat revealing
For their heart may bear the marks
Of what they once were feeling
So, please handle it with care and treat it with respect
And in return, turn in your heart for them to inspect

LOVING
Poems for an Awesome! Life

Like Nothing Else

Missing you…
Makes my heart hurt
Loving you…
Makes my heart grow!

And when I'm holding you
It makes my soul so happy
So Happy!
Like nothing else in the world Can, ever Has, or ever Will

You ask me if I MISS You?
My LOVE, all I want to do is be WITH you

In My Arms

Please let me be your safe place
In my arms, may you always find peace
Please find sanctuary in my company
Where you can always feel at ease

Please find shelter in my harbor
Your calm reality in a horrible storm
Your secure hideaway to escape
To feel cozy comfortable and warm

And when you ever may need comfort
From life's imperfect times
And you need strong arms to hold you
I pray to our maker you'll choose mine

4 Foot Bed

Cold and snowy winter night, all nestled in a nice warm bed
Dressed in cozy warm PJ's, ultra-soft pillows for our heads

Everything is calm; everything is nice
Perfect preparation for a wonderfully peaceful night!!!

What the......!!
Is that your feet?

They are sooo cold!!!
They have chilled me to the bottom of my soul!

Wow, they are frigid! You used to be sweet!
Why did you disturb me with those ice-cold feet!??

What...what did you say?

You need my help to get warm?
Without me, you could not possibly get through this storm?

Why didn't you say so...let me warm up those ice-blocks
When you talk so sweet to me, there's no need for socks!

So Needy

Did you ever need something so bad?
Not having it made you sad
Thinking of it made you glad

Wanting it made you nuts
No 'ifs', 'ands' or 'buts'

You feel your heart is breaking
And your bones start really aching

You are really feeling lonely
You start wondering..."If only..."

Then somehow-somewhere you get a little bite
And it feels so right

Your head starts to spin
And you can't contain your grin

And your heart grows a size
Like you just won a prize

It really is something
When your heart gets what it's wanting!

Carousel

When I close my eyes I see you
Like your face and essence are forever etched in my eyelids
A natural slideshow of beauty
I know your face so well by now...
No further evidence is needed
So, let's keep it coming
I don't want this show to stop!

Keep It Coming

I want to make you happier and healthier
And wealthier than you've ever been before

And I'm extremely optimistic about
What our future holds in store

So, I hope you like what I'm selling you
And that you'll keep coming back for more!

Love Bone

Within our body, it seems we are diverse
Of course, we have the obvious:
The stomach, the brain, the heart
And all kinds of little parts

Just the same
Let's not forget the bones
They add structure to our frame

Some are strong and make us tall
Some are big and some are small
And of some you don't even know the names at all

Now, please allow me to introduce a new bone
Of which you never hear
A bone I just discovered
A bone that just appeared
A bone that seems to react whenever you are near

No, it's not the wish bone - "Y?"
It's for the birds, not us
And No, it's not the funny bone
It has too much nerve to be humerus

The bone I am introducing is a bone
That keeps the spirit whole
A bone that runs from the top of your head
Down to the bottom of your sole

It's the bone that amazes
The bone that seeks passion
It's the bone that starts crazes
The bone that's always in fashion

I call it the 'Love Bone'
'Why?' you say?
To explain it to you is merely child's play:
When I see you, it makes me smile
When I smell you, it makes me excited
When I hear you, it makes me alert
And when I'm with you, it makes me delighted

It's the most powerful bone in the body, I'm sure
Because it functions so natural and so pure
My Love Bone is connected to the....everything!
There is frankly no detour

Quite simply:
You know how to treat me
Better than anyone I have ever known
And now I understand why
I have come to discover My Love Bone

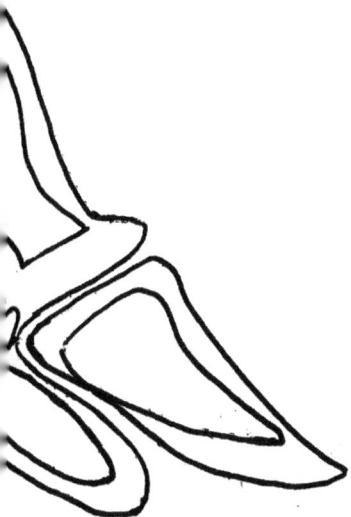

The Gift

"I gave you my heart"...That's just what she said
Those sweet sweet words chimed softly in my head

My knees got weak, soon after she stated it
A flood of love flowed over me when she articulated it

"I gave you my heart" did I hear her right?
Those words weighed in heavy, yet they came out so light

I saw the sounds leave her lips as she said them
Forever in my mind I plan to imbed them

I will never forget what she said...
I swear

There is no better way to tell someone...
Just how deeply you care

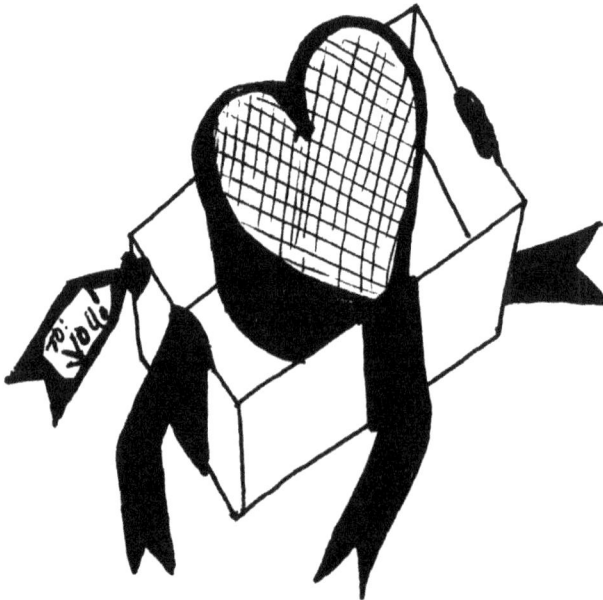

Do You Dream Of Me?

Tell me, what am I like in your dreams?

Am I handsome? Am I tall?
Am I funny? Am I small?

Am I smiling? Do I laugh?
Do I smell good?
Like I am fresh from the bath?

Am I fit? Am I slim?
How's my hair look?
Do I need a trim?

Am I pale?
Or Am I tanned?
Do I have jeans on?
If so, what's the brand?

Am I wild? Am I polite?
How are my eyes?
Clear and bright?

How am I dressed?
Overall, are you impressed?

Tell me, tell me, don't you tease me!
Tell me what I'm like in your dreams
Yes, that would please me :)

The exact details of your dreams maybe no one knows
At least tell me one thing...

"Am I wearing any clothes?"

You Are Sick?

You poor thing
I heard you are sick.....
Don't feel down
'Cause I know a trick

Yes, let's get you WELL fast!
No time to wait
Big things are coming
And it will be great!

So, breathe lots of fresh air
Not too cold ...nor too hot
Get lots of Vitamin C
Chicken soup can help tons...I'll go whip you up a pot

Now, rest in bed all day
That's right, that's what I said
That's where you should stay
Relaxed in your bed

And nothing helps more
When your nose is real runny
Then tons and tons of movies
Especially if they are funny!

So giggle, laugh and smile
That's what you need when you are down
And if you need more to be happy about
Then I'll come around!

My Turn!

Now I am sick
And you are the well one
I am weak
And you are the swell one

It was hard for us, when you were sick
And I brought the cheer
Now, you are all healthy and I just lay here

Sweating and Sneezing
and Runny-nosing and Aching
and Head-aching and not Sleeping
and Seeping and Weeping

Let's stop this cycle now
Don't ask me how
Let's find a trick
To make both of us NOT sick

Yes, both of us happy
Both of us strong
Both of us ... at the same time
Let's not take too long

We are too Awesome to be down
We need to be UP
We are too active to be nursing ills
Too healthy to be popping pills

Yes, let's be healthy together
Same time, Same place
Then I can truly enjoy
The beautiful smile on your face

Help!

Head over heels
I'm falling

Rolling, bouncing
I'm really hauling...

Down the hill so fast I'm falling
With no signs of stalling

It's your name I'm calling
The whole time I'm falling

I should be bawling
With the incredible speed I'm falling
Like I'm beach-balling

However, I'm just so happy
And it's not some small thing

Head over heels
I'm falling
And it's enthralling!

Let's Roll!

Loving with hearts..whole
That's how we roll

Allowing our hearts to grow
That's how we roll

Respect and admiration
That's the goal

Making each other happy:)
That's how we roll

Getting together with time we stole
That's how we roll

No need for a remote control
That's how we roll

In the park...In the wild...
Taking a stroll
That's how we roll

Center on the positive things in life
Create solutions for any strife
Not allowing stress to take its toll
That's how we roll

Focus on being Awesome!
With healthy and smiling souls
That's how we roll

Own It!

You really belong to me
I feel it

In the way you make me feel
It's unreal

In the way you move
When we are in the groove

In the way you speak
It makes my knees weak

In your eyes
My hopes give rise

Your love overflows on me from your soul
The way you pour it

You really belong to me
And I love you for it!

All Ears

When you whisper in my ear
I can never hear it

It just tickles me so much!
Every time you go near it

19

Your Stuff

Your hair
Your eyes
Your face
Your lips

Your neck
Your arms
Your fingertips

Your heart
Your brain
Your soul
Your style

Your laughs
Your jokes
Your winks
Your smiles

I don't know if you work hard
At being awesomely beautiful all day
To me, it seems you're just built that way!

I'm Sure Of It!

I'm sure your parents knew
How wonderful you'd be when you grew

I'm sure they always saw how successful you'd be
And how you'd grow to be caring, kind, loving and sweet

And today, I'm sure they know this to be true...

Do you?

Dream On!

Dream of me
      When you are away
Dream of me
      When you are alone
Dream of me
      When you are traveling
Dream of me
      When you are home

Dream of me
      When you are scared
Dream of me
      When you are pleased too
Dream of me
      When you are in a crowd
Dream of me
      When you need to

Dream of me
      In the night
Dream of me
      During daybreak
Dream of me
      Whenever you're able
Dream of me
      Every chance you can take

Dream of me
      When you're doubting
Dream of me
      When you're believing
It's not too much, don't worry
      I dream of you each time I'm breathing!

Let's Make Magic!

Gather around! Yes, yes of course you!
There's something I want to show to you

It's something you've only read about
Or maybe even have dreamed about
So, let me show you what it's all about

There's nothing up my sleeve
No smoke, no tricks, no mirrors
So, please don't hold back, yes in fact,
please come nearer

When it happens it will be fast, like the BLINK of an eye
Or even a WINK of an eye
And the only ones that will see it, are here together
Yes, you and I

OK, so here's what I want to show you, are you ready?
Please pay attention and try to stay steady

Close your eyes:
This is something you won't want to MISS!

(SURPRISE!!! It's a Kiss!:)

I'm Gonna Love You With Everything

Darling, when I think of you:

My toes begin to curl
And my hair stands at attention
My skin starts to tingle
In places too odd to mention

My nose starts to sniff
And My eyes start to water
And My hearts beatin'
7 times faster than it oughter

My arms start to reach out
For it's you they want to squeeze
My legs, wanna run to you
Their getting sweaty at the knees

My palms start to heat up
And my stomach's in a knot
And there's a HUGE smile on my face
When usually, there's not

Sweetheart, I love you so
I feel my heart's about to burst
It's too late to stop it now
I'm not afraid of getting hurt

Where's this emotion come from?
I just may never know
So, I'm gonna love you BIG
And see where it all goes!

I'm gonna love you with everything
Since we've been together my heart wants to sing
I found beauty in my life
With all that magic that you bring
I'm gonna love you with everything

Meet Me On The Moon

Let's get stranded in space. How about on the moon!
First, we will make a table out of moon-rocks
And then we'll sip green tea at noon

Then, we can hold hands and take a walk
Around a crater's crown
Wearing heavy space boots to weigh us all down

And remember to bring the crackers please
Just in case the moon is really made of cheese

And I'll bring the juice, yes, I know you adore it
Let's be careful it won't float away
When we start to pour it

We'll make huge promises under the earth-light
And we'll shout big wishes to a star
When it twinkles back, the wish will be granted
No matter how incredible they are

It seems ultra-clear that our time
Is a very special present
And it's up to us to live it!
So, let's be fearless
And make awesome and powerful requests
For the Universe will be happy to give it!

Essentially Mine

You, my Love, are living in my mind
Your essence is embedded in everything that I do
Each thought, each word, each movement I make
Is conceived while dreaming of You

It is impossible to separate You
From my every living moment
I'm longing for You
And deeply missing you when you are not near
You have become an incredibly special part of who I am
And everything about you
Yes everything,
I hold unfathomably dear

Everything that I love to do
I wonder if you'd love to do it too
Every bite of food that I savor
I question whether you too would enjoy the flavor

When I sleep, I dream of us being together
Holding hands, slowly strolling through life forever

And when I'm awake
I'm planning glorious around-the-world
Adventurous rendezvous
No suitcases needed
The only thing we need to pack is one me and one you

It's uncontested, the depth of the love we have forged
For every second we spend together
Leaves an unquenchable thirst for more!

Diagnosis

My lips are throbbing all day long

My sense of taste has completely gone

I explained to the doctor my issue over the phone

He said that YOU definitely gave me a rare case

Of Imustkissyamora Syndrome

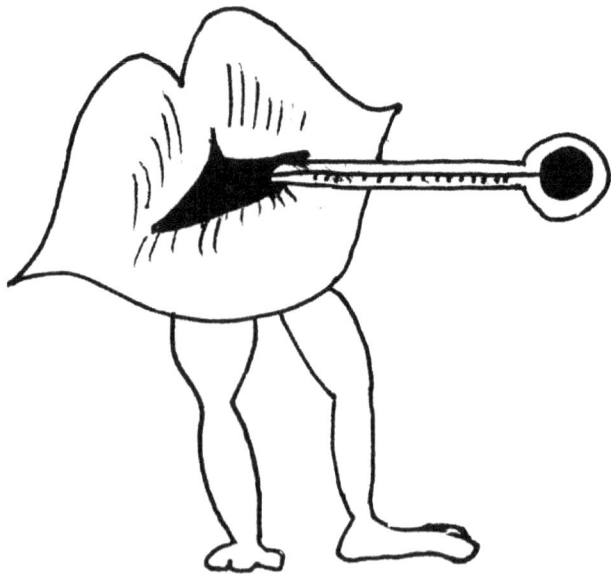

U R A KEEPER

I'm never gonna let you go
        Nothing will make me do it
I'm gonna hold on to you forever
        It's easy, there's nothing to it!

I'm never gonna let you go
        And I'm gonna handle you just right
I'm gonna hold on to you forever
        Not too loose, not too tight

I'm never gonna let you go
        I may make mistakes along the way
I'm gonna hold on to you forever
        So, please let me be there for you
        Each and every day

I'm never gonna let you go
        You are my top priority
I'm gonna hold on to you forever
        You are number one, then comes me

I'm never gonna let you go
        I'm in so deep; I have to go all the way
I'm gonna hold on to you forever
        Please say its "OK"!

I'm never gonna let you go
        When you need me, I will be there
I'm gonna hold on to you forever
        And I'll be super duper devoted, I swear!

All Better

Ouch!
You hit me right where it hurts!
Right where all my sensitivities gather hot!
It's exactly where, to be hit, I'd rather not!

All my insecurities and tears
Are gathered there in that place of fears
And you had to hit me right there
Seemingly without worry, evidently without care

My heart is racing!!!
My hands are sweaty!!!!
My......Ahhhhh, you kissed me!?
And you said the sweetest "I'm sorry!"
Well, that feels better already!!!!!

FYI

If you are waiting for me to let you go
------- Don't

If you want me to say goodbye
------- I won't

If you are expecting me not to care
------ Stop right now!

If you want me to stop loving you
--------I can't, I just don't know how!

Tears For Sale

Tears for sale!
Buy one pair get 2!

So many tears have fallen from my eyes already
I don't know what else to do!

Tears for sale!
Get them while they're wet!

The love of my life just told me goodbye
And now I'm so very upset!

Tears for sale!
Why she left me I'll never know

Oh wait...she's back!!!!!!!...

She only left to change her clothes!
......This shop is now CLOSED!

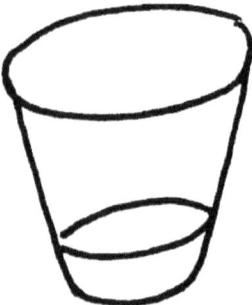

Facing Time

I can't wait for the time that's coming so soon
When its midnight, I'm already wishing it was noon!

I know you should never wish your time away
It's just impossible for me to think any other way

So, let's speed up the clock
Just this once, til we get there
And then we will slooooowwww it down
And not go anywhere

Ah, to be able to speed up time
Then slow it down…
That would be the best
Nothing could top it
Unless…, when we are together
We can figure out just how we can stop it!

Puppet Master

I like to be the puppet master
Controlling all the movements
Pulling all the strings
The manipulator of moving things

If you would be my marionette
You would certainly make me
The happiest puppeteer yet

If you'd allow me to hold the wires
Of that, I'd never tire

I'll admire you from every angle
And keep your wires free from tangles

We'll play out adventures in our own unique styles
Ending each daily performance full of beautiful smiles

Together, we will make a wonderful play
One that would be appreciated
From ancient times until today

And the whole world can cheer
Of the articulation we have accomplished here

Since we have met, you have revealed the real me
You've opened my eyes both vertically and horizontally

You've unveiled a whole new world for me to see
So, it's natural that it's only you I trust now
To lead me where you want me to be

And here's the pièce de résistance of our special art:
I want to switch parts!

Here are all my strings, you now control my parts
Please be MY puppet master, anytime you want, you may start

One request, be please careful with the 7th string!
(That one controls my heart)

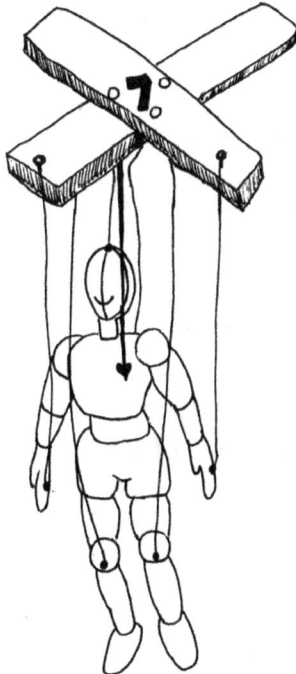

Puzzle Partner

Now, just look at the size of our Puzzle!
It has so many shapes, sizes, twists and turns in it!
To solve this puzzle through
To its glorious completion
We will really have to be earnin' it!

There are times the sheer size of it
May seem a wee bit frightening
And at times it may be haunting us
To complete all the connections
May at times appear nearly impossible
It's the beautiful realization of putting
It all together that keeps taunting us

Looking at all the pieces,
Lying haphazard on the table
Can leave a person questioning if
He is ultimately able
To navigate the endless combinations,
And all the loose ends to lock
All these challenges in the way,
Trying to hinder, confuse and block

Perhaps, it is best not to look
At all the permutations
That would just cause a myriad of fru
To tackle these puzzle pieces,
Let's focus first on a few
Yes, let's just start with two

Two little pieces making the perfect connection
Putting them together fills my heart with affection
There, that feels great, that was a great initial tes
Now, let's tackle the rest!

We will start by the obvious,
Turning all the pieces upward facing
Making piles of commonalities
With appreciation and embracing
Then while constructing the outer edges,
The framework will appear before our eyes
Yes, when the outline is done,
Our souls will soon rise

Next, let's discover the similarities,
Perfect fits and the parts that match alike
Knowing that our perfect picture is now within sight
The parts are beginning to align!
Surely, this is a sign!

Together, we will begin to visualize what we can achieve
A clear picture of what we will conceive
Excitement will be flooding our veins
Racing through our hearts like high-speed trains

Stay with me, we will work on this puzzle bit by bit
And we will show the world how we made it all fit

One day we will laugh at this,
We will be rolling on the floor
At how difficult this puzzle looked at the start,
We won't have to doubt it anymore
A tremendous pile of ambiguity
Will be overcome with ingenuity!

We will face this challenge…One designed to amuse
And we will win it over
With a loving and patient effort
The universe surely won't refuse

So, let's keep tackling this puzzle together
Even if it takes forever
For we know one day we will be smiling
After we've mastered all the tiling

You Got Soul, Mate

You make me BE the ME,
And SEE the ME,
That I always wanted ME to BE.

Voyage

Please allow me now to tell you a tale (it even rhymes)
Of two people who leave their pasts behind

They secured their hopes to a post
With heavy-duty ropes

On an island surrounded by sharks and icy-rough seas
And they left together on a boat
Built for a one-way journey
Filled with only You's and Me's

Priming For The Climbing

Well, here we are
In front of this enormous mountain!
I'm so excited you are up for this climb!
I have to warn you, it may take some time

For us to reach the top
We can never stop
We have to keep moving step by step, day by day
Let's start right now and we'll be on our way!

When it gets really difficult and treacherous
Let's stay together
Let's not allow the conditions to get the best of us

There are some parts of the climb that are steep
And some canyons that may run deep

There may be times when our footing is cracking
We can get through it no problem
After all, it's each other we are backing

Please take my hand, and let's keep a nice grip
Not too loose, not too tight, let's not let it slip

We are also tethered together with this special binding
Made of the strongest stuff in the universe worth finding

It's invisible you can't be seeing it
Don't worry, it's there, just believe in it

For safety let's review:
On this trip, it's only us two
We have to stick together
No matter what the weather
Take my hand, Keep a nice grip
Never let it slip
Have faith and trust
Success is a must

So, we are agreed!
Awesome! Because this is exactly what we both need
We have climbed almost halfway there already
We should keep going
We were enjoying the trip so much
We got all the way here fast! Without even knowing!

And the secret that you may not yet have heard
Is that the view from the top
Is beautiful beyond words
And although only the patient
And most special pairs ever get to view it
The good news is, from my perspective...
The universe truly wants us to do it!

Dream Book

I've just read an unusual page from our dream book
And now I can't sleep
That was quite a surprising twist
With emotions running deep

Here I am now, staring at the ceiling
Not exactly sure what I'm thinking or what I'm feeling
Looking up from my bed, with this fear of the unknowing
Afraid for my next move
Unsure the direction the wind may be blowing

I've counted all the spiders
I've counted every dust ball
I've counted all the cracks
While I'm here, flat on my back

I'm thinking of today
I'm thinking of all my yesterdays
I'm thinking of my many tomorrows
All layered in happiness and sorrows

I've tried the warm milk trick
I've tried breathing techniques
I've tried counting sheep
I just can't fall asleep

There's no light in the room
There's no sound keeping me alert
Tonight, in the sky just one star
Holding all my dreams, taking me afar

I think it's time to let go of the fears
That must be what keeps waking me
I think it's time to count my blessings
At how happy you are making me

Sometimes our dream book can be a terrifying adventure
And you try to skip to the end of the chapter
Yet, it's better to dream of happiness
And turn the pages together, and see what comes after

You Stayed

You've seen me cranky
You've seen me proud
You've seen me quiet
And you've seen me loud

You've seen me in good times
You've seen me in bad
You've seen me happy
And you've seen me sad

You've seen me on my best days
You've seen me on my worst
You've seen me come in last
And you've seen me come in first

You've seen me go crazy
You've seen me stay calm
You've seen me gentle as a butterfly
And you've seen me explode like a bomb

And even through all these sights
You were here right by my side
And even when, I thought I may have scared you away
You stayed

Finding You

I looked all night for the right route to take
That would lead me right into your heart
I found so many connections
Yet, I didn't know where to start

There were fast lanes and slow lanes
High-flying airplanes and locomotive trains
There were balloons and kites
And two-wheeled bikes

So many ways to go
They were just all too slow!

The route I took at last was simple...and fine
In fact, it works all the time

To get to see you the quickest
All I have to do is close my eyes
And your beautiful image is what my heart provides

My soul knows you so well;
I can find you even in the dimmest of lighting
To have you so close to my heart...is truly exciting

Cost Of Love

"If I love you as much as my
heart leads me to believe,
then why does it hurt
SO MUCH every time that
you leave?"

"Well Sweetheart, Our love is so
plentiful its flowing over the edges
of our hearts. So, the price we must
pay for loving so deeply is
in the time we are
apart"

Through My Eyes

If you could see YOU
Through the thankful eyes that I DO
You'd see instantly and forever,
What I already know is true

The radiance of beauty that glows all around your being
The peacefulness that you bring to my life
Is what you'd be seeing

Lips full with truthfulness,
Mouthing tenderness without trying
Eyes ripe with adventure, is what you'd be spying

A smile that brings me happiness, a heart that beats pure
My favorite person in the world,
Making me long to have more

The star of my thoughts, filling my days and my nights
With shooting stars, sunrises and life's greatest delights

If you could see YOU
Through the fortunate eyes that I DO
You'd see immeasurably and exactly just how much I love you

Monster!

You have created a Monster my Dear!
You are the creator and it's only Master, that's clear!

Your Monster has a ferocious smile and an enormous heart
With a laugh so big, it's right off the chart!

A Monster with giant hugging arms,
Who purrs soothing sounds
You have created a Monster who only has UPs!
(Never any downs)
Your Monster says the sweetest words and
Has a peacefulness that's screaming
And its entire day is spent daydreaming

A Monster with big ears for listening
For the songs that you sing
And a sensitive nose for the flowery smells that you bring

You have created a Monster my Dear!
So, please hold its hand and keep it quite near!

Alternate Endings:

1. And it comes out to play every time you appear!
2. Now it's up to you to keep it alive, don't let it disappear!
3. So, just kiss it a lot and give it some beer!
4. It will love you, and protect you, so have no fear!

Heartbeats

They say that a person's heart
Will beat 3 Billion times before it's through

Now, I don't know for sure if that's true
I really don't have a clue

What I do know is that I want to spend
All my remaining heartbeats loving YOU

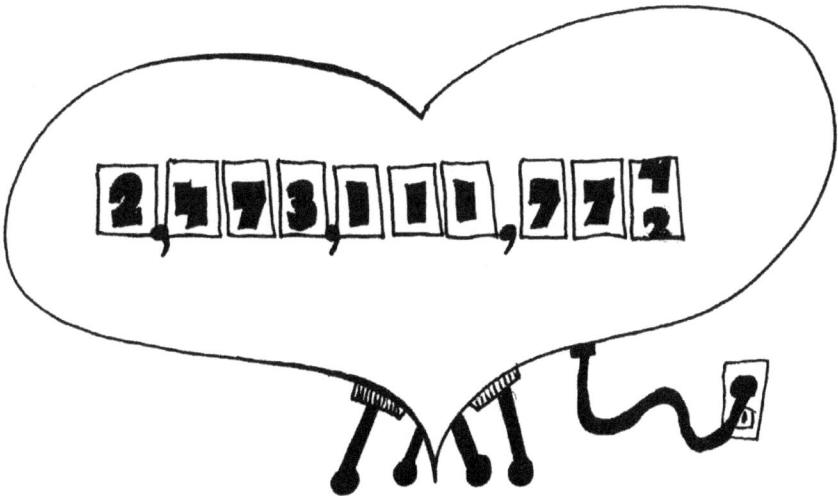

Super Duper

When YOU are able to give ME your precious time
That's when I'm feeling my best!
That's when I'm able to bounce bullets of my chest!

I'm Flying High and Feeling Tough!
You know 'Man of Steel' kind of stuff!

When you are busy and can't make the time
For the smallest of little things for me
It's like kryptonite to my soul
And it does all funny things to me

It makes me lose my powers, and it weakens my might
I'm grounded, I'm vulnerable and it blurs my sight

You can inspire me to fly over tall buildings
And fly faster than a bullet!
So, when you are able, please take just a moment for me
There's really nothing to it!

Super-Villains are out to steal our smiles
And time is moving faster, that's true
Better to Champion a heroic moment
For someone who means the Universe to you

So, whenever you can
Please provide the BOOM! POW! and BANG! to my lifeline
I'll be your real-life Super Hero!
And you can be mine!

Rare Please:

Sometimes I may not listen very well
Sometimes I may act out of place
Sometimes I may not say the right things
Sometimes I may not succeed in keeping
A smile on your beautiful face

Sometimes I may not seem right in the head
Sometimes I may come across kind of rough
Sometimes I may not do what I should
Sometimes I may not consider your feelings enough

Please don't let those rare times fool you
Or cast a shadow on my being
This is not who I really am
You know this is not the real me you are seeing

These are the times I may need you more than ever
Please believe in me
Because it's your faith that I treasure

And I promise to forever be open and honest and true
And I promise that I'll be the best friend you ever knew

Sleep Well

When you really love someone

Unconditionally trusting them

Is the right thing to do

When you do that

Sleeping peacefully

Will be an every single night thing for you

Silver Lining

When it's dark and rainy
And the weather is crappy

Share an umbrella with someone you love
And you'll always be happy

Love Seeds

Today, my very best friend gave me
This special pack of seeds
She said, "When they grow to their fullest;
They will provide all we need"

She assured me, "Growing them will be easy
There's really nothing to it"
So, allow me to read the instructions out loud
And let's see how to do it:

Step 1: Plant your seeds with care
Anyway, anytime, anywhere

Step 2: Cover them with hugs
Allow them take deep roots over time
If you are excited about the daily growth
That's already a great sign!

Step 3: Feed them with kisses, winks,
Stories and long walks
Then add honesty, truthfulness,
Yummy food and open talks

Step 4: Smile as you watch them grow
Every night and every single day
Protect them from harm...
From every which way

Step 5: Bathe your seeds in bright sunshine
And handle them gently and kind
Please, be sure to keep them warm
Wrapped in all the tenderness you can find

Step 6: Talk sweet words to your seeds
That you are now growing
And they will rise taller than the mountains! How high?
Well, there's just no way of knowing!

Step 7: The fruit of your attention
Will be an endless bounty
When you do it just right
Its juicy sweetness with the love of your life!

This is super exciting, I must say!
I'm going to get on this right away!

This is going to get the full attention
From My Heart, My Body and My Mind!
And I'm going to share the harvest with her
One delicious bite at a time!

Snow Day

I've officially declared a snow day today
The storm will be amazing! That's what the predictions say!

So, let's gather up some fun, some food and some drink
And what else will we need? Hmm, let me think:

We'll watch some old movies and let's break out that puzzle
We'll build a big fire and to keep warm we can nuzzle

Let's light some bright candles
With our own perfect matches
So, get on your PJ'S and we will batten down the hatches

The stores are off limits, so are the banks and the shops
We don't need much more; we've already got quite a lot!

A snow-day-buddy is the most important person to choose
I hope you pick me, because I definitely pick you!

Your best snow day buddy should be your soul-mate
Your love and/or your best friend
You are all three for me
So, I'm hoping this snow day will never end!

Walk With Me, Talk With Me

How exciting!
We have now passed the point of "NO TURNING AROUND"
There's never been a point in our lives before
That's as happy as this new happiness we found

From here, we'll keep moving forward
Let's continue to build our dreams
Because right now the new love filling our old hearts
Is bursting them right at the seams

So, come walk with me, talk with me
Come hold my hand
Over mountains, over fields of grass
With our feet in the sand

So, come walk with me, talk with me
There's just no turning 'round
Because nothing in our old life
Compares with this new life we've found!

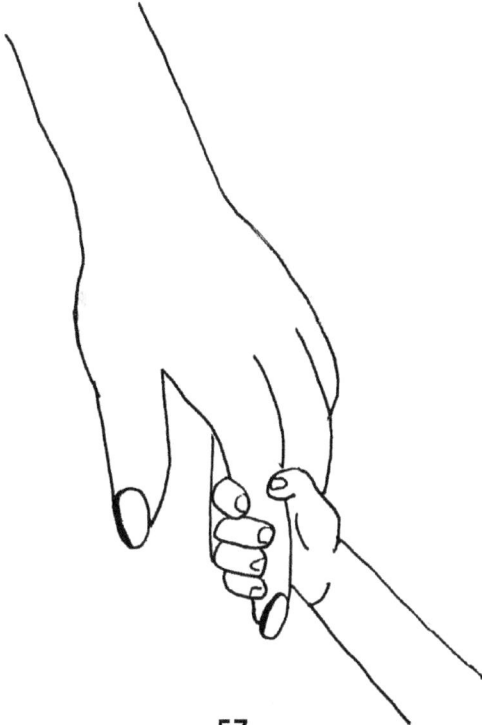

Easy Peasy

Sweetheart,
The way you fill up my heart with love
I just have no clue how you do it

It seems to come so easy for you
Like there's really nothing to it!

Sometimes...

You say that you really love me
And you'll stay with me 'till the end of time
Then, I must tell you a few things about me
A few things for you to keep in mind:

Sometimes my breath smells
And sometimes I may fart
And sometimes when I have something to do
I may not know where to start
And...

Sometimes my face in the morning
May seem wrinkled creased and old
And sometimes I may be cranky
If I'm too hot, too tired or too cold
And...

Sometimes I may seem lazy
And sometimes I may not make a proper meal
And sometimes I may be scared
To tell you exactly how I feel
And...

Sometimes I may not exercise
And sometimes you'll find me just relaxing on the couch
And sometimes I may eat popcorn so fast
That I may completely miss my mouth
So...

If after reading all of this
You still want to stick around
Then I believe that means you'll love me forever
So, let's get excited about settling down!

Pull It Together

When your body is in one place
And your soul is in another
Your heart may feel less than whole
Waiting for the one half to join the other

And when the two parts are finally joined
You will find your heart has grown bigger
From where it had started
For once united,
The pieces will have strengthened their bond
Refusing again to ever be parted

Let's Make That Deal!

It's the deal of a lifetime
An offer you can't refuse
So incredibly Awesome!
It's something you'll love to use

It's a truly unique opportunity...
It's yours for the takin'
So, believe it with all your heart
It's pure magic in the makin'

You're taking home the trophies
You've put yourself at the top
Your train is racing down the tracks
With no signs of a stop

You've earned the right to win
You put your ALL in this race
And how can I tell all this about you?
Well, just look at your smiling face!

My Fortune Told

I went to a fortune teller's shop last night
And I asked her to show me MY future
She led me down a long hallway
And left me in a bright and cheerful room
After a moment she reappeared in her clairvoyant costume

She chanted and sang as she began her reading
(I didn't exactly know where this was leading)
To be honest
I was a little scared and very excited
Hoping she was genuinely authentic and divinely sighted

For a few minutes
I began to wonder if anything would happen at all
It seemed an eternity as I sat there
Wishing that the universe would answer her call
Then she finally told me to look into her crystal ball!
Right there before my eyes
It was my future I saw!

And do you know what came into view?
Do you want to know what finally came through?
I'm dying to tell you
Because I believe this is 100% true!
The crystal clear image in my future
Was a beautiful picture of you!

Do The Math

My face is smiling
My heart beats strong
My mouth feels like singing and whistling all day long

My nightly dreams are so wonderful
And my daydreams are even better
Like the one where I write "I'm So Happy!"
On a billboard in GIANT CAPITAL LETTERS!

The universe seems so peaceful
The world seems perfectly right
And the stars have a special twinkle tonight

Everything makes sense
And all the love songs sound perfectly true
If my calculations are correct
This adds up to (Love = I + YOU!)

The Bridge

Did you hear the news?
They are building a bridge from the Old World to the New!
Reuniting relatives, family and friends
And putting all the borders finally to an end

It's a massive new bridge that crosses oceans and time
A link that brings together
All the best you can possibly find

I saw them pour the foundations in the shape of a heart
And I thought to myself, "What a perfect way to start!"

Soon, this bridge will unite people of all kinds
From all times
And new conversations will start
And no one will ever again be kept apart

A bridge with new walkways beaming with wonder
And all beasts will be welcome
To walk along, fly over or swim under

The world will once again be joined together
From the powers that once parted it
So, let us now hold hands and rejoice
For finally they started it!

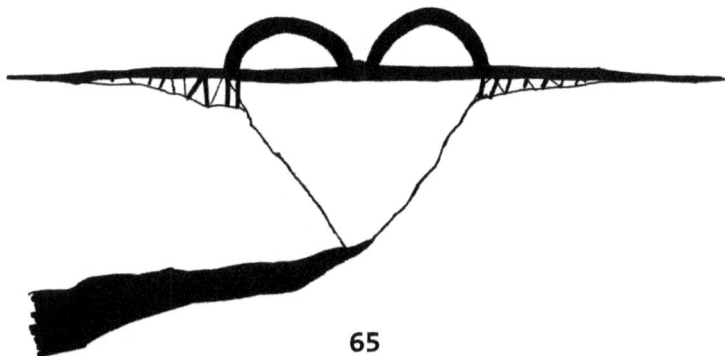

Ice Cold

Share your coldest fears with your Best Friend
And they will melt away like summer ice

Electric Wrap

Your love has now completely surrounded me
Exciting and comforting
(Like a fabulous disco blanket)

I'm going to wrap it around us while we dance
Then softly whisper "I love you" to your heart
(So I can properly thank it)

The Wringer

Sometimes I feel like the end of the world is coming soon
Even though I know that it's not true
It feels like I'll lose myself for sure
Until I realize what I found when I found you

My heart can seem so tight
Like it's being squeezed in a wringer
Stress races through it and it beats way too fast
Until I think about the ring I put on your finger

As a reminder for our love
I slowly crafted the circle of gold
And once it was forged and cooled
It was time to forever break the mould

I imagine that I sometimes I can get tense over nothing
Because I don't want to lose you
After all, how often do you find a love
That's so beautiful, so genuine and so true?

So, I'll just wait for the dark cloud to pass
Trusting that you will take care of my heart forever
Replacing my fears with memories of sweet precious times
For we can beat any challenge in front of us
As long as we face it together

Communication Lines

The communication lines seemed all distorted today
We couldn't hear what the other person was trying to say

You'd say something sweet
And I could only hear beep-beep!
I'd say something nice
And you'd ask me to repeat it twice, repeat it twice!

Well, I think it's perfectly fine
To rarely misalign
You tried your best
And I tried mine

Let's trust in our love and then
Tomorrow we can start over again
Come to think of it...
I know what can make our communication much better...
Let's just be together!!!

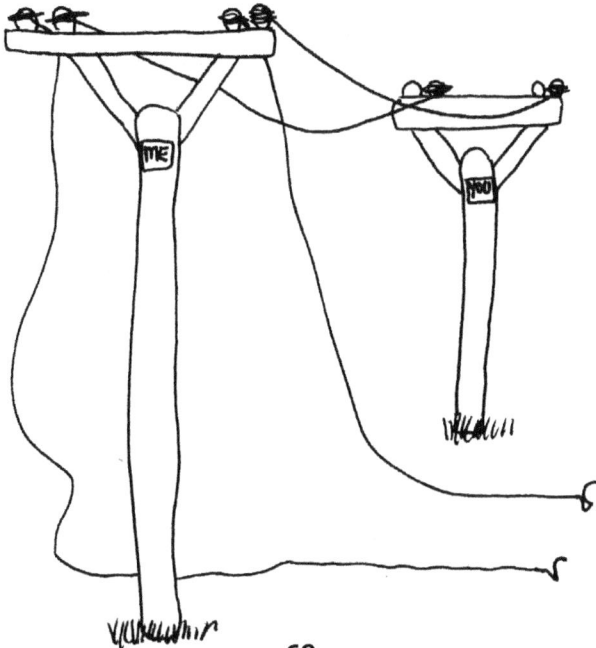

Talking To My Puppy

My favorite jeans have a rip!
I need somewhere to send them
I need someone to care and sew and stitch and mend them

What will I do without 'em?
I feel my best when I'm in 'em

When I wear them I feel comfortable, confident and strong
I won't be able to live without them long!

Let me slide them on and show you
While I figure out what to do

What did you say?
You like them this way?

With the worn-in-legs
And rips in the trim?
The broken-in-look,
You say it makes me look slim?

Well then
If that's the way you feel
If I am to believe what you say

Then there's no need
To mend sew or stitch them
Because, actually,
I feel the same way!

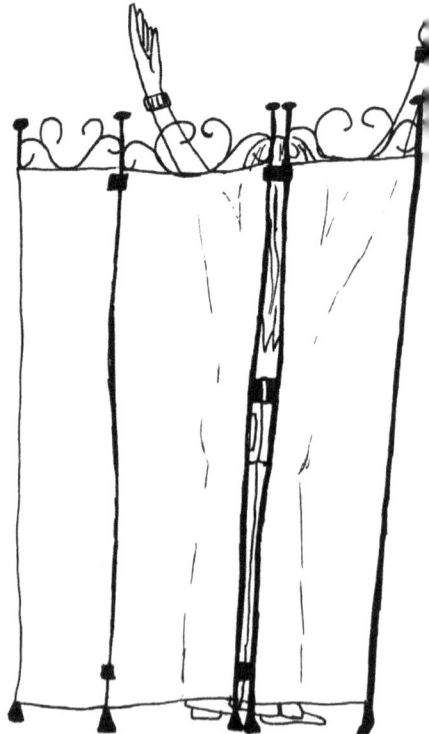

Olive Yoo

Olive Yoo (sounds like "Boo!") was a very happy girl...
She may have been the happiest girl in the world!

Olive Yoo smiled all the day long
For in Olive's life, nothing could ever go wrong

For no matter where she ever would appear
If there was someone who knew her near
They would always walk up or call:
"Olive Yoo!" and she would stand 10 feet tall

Yes, no matter what the time or where the place
Just say her name
and Olive Yoo will have a big smile on her face

The Promise

There's a promise I made to myself
By myself, to myself, a long long time ago
And that's to always believe in myself
No matter how rough things may go

A promise to have conviction in my convictions
A promise to believe in my beliefs
A promise to be the best me I can be
A promise to achieve what I'm meant to achieve

And when I start to doubt myself, by myself
I think back to that promise I made to myself
Like an old friend, my solid foundation
And the belief in that promise erases my frustration

I take that time
I make that time
To remember the promise I made to myself
To put my inner peacefulness above everything else

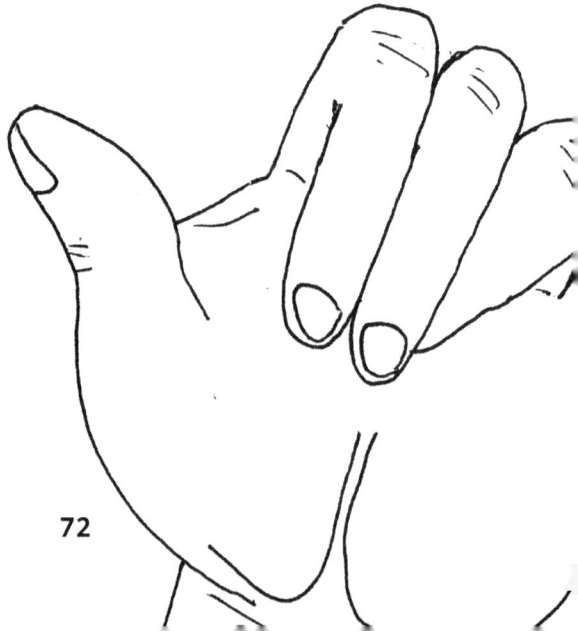

For whatever is to be is to be
And my own happiness is up to no one else, just me

Its only one life (at a time) we are given
Its only one life (at a time) that we are living

So, let's forgive ourselves, and forgive the others
Let's enjoy our friendships and love our mothers

And when the shadow of doubt starts to sneak on in
When you start to question your own heart
It's time to review that promise you made to yourself
It may be the perfect time to make a brand new start

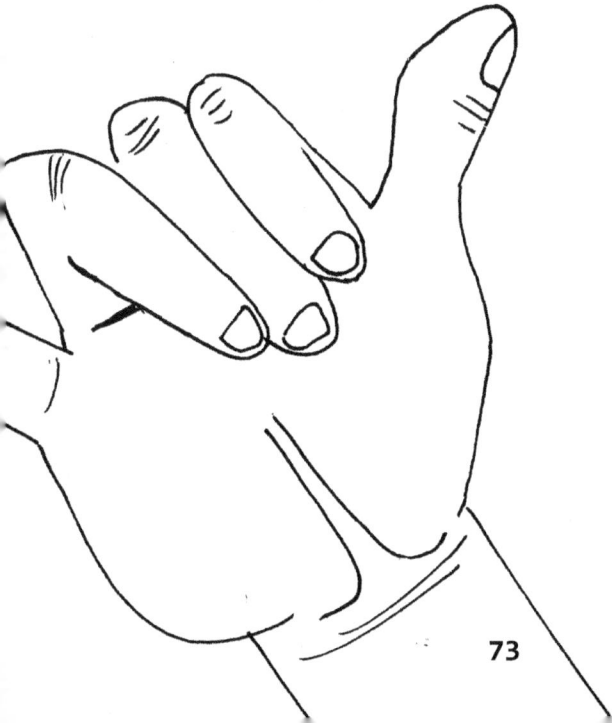

Happy "Day Before" Day!

Tomorrow's Your Birthday!
I have a smile I can't stop
I want to scream out "I love You!"
From the highest mountaintop

For tomorrow is a celebration of YOU
And all that you are
Wonderful affectionate beautiful caring creative smart..
This list can go far!

Tomorrow's your Birthday
So get ready for the attention
The calls, the gifts, the notes and the posts
From family & friends (too many to mention!)

I feel so happy.....…and it's for you!
You'll get so much love the day after today
So today, I want you to KNOW that I love you
And that everything will be Super-Duper-OK!

There is nothing I can wrap and give you
To show you how much you mean to me
There is not a ribbon big enough to wrap up our fire
No box I can find that can contain our desire

On your very special "day before" day
We can meet in old places
Or new places
Or very sunny beach places

And it's awesome what we CAN DO
And what will forever be true...
Is together, we will live the moments
Before, after and on
Your very special "day before" days
To share the meaning of the words
I Love YOU!

I Love You For You

I know one thing that is 100 percent true
I love You for You

You see, I love all the little things that you do
And I love the big things too

I love you when you are happy
And I love you when you're feeling blue

I love you so much
I wanna scream out "WoooHooo!"

And I promise to stick to you like glue
Without any hullabaloo

I just have no clue
What I'd do without you

Our love started off small
And then it grew

and grew

and grew!

At first, I loved one thing about you
Then it became a billion and two!

What can I say? What can I do?
I just love you for you!

Possibilities

All you need is that one person
that truly believes in you

And you can move mountains
And swim oceans!

About the Author

J. Leone is the author-artist of the 3 part series Living, Laughing and Loving, Poems for an Awesome! Life.

He is a private business owner, a writer of songs and available for public speaking.

He can be spotted in Awesome! places like New York City; Princeton, NJ; Miami, FL; Amsterdam, The Netherlands and on the beautiful Caribbean island of St. Maarten.

GreenSpring
greenspringnv@gmail.com

.

www.ingramcontent.com/pod-product-compliance
Lightning Source LLC
Chambersburg PA
CBHW071838020426
42331CB00007B/1778